Mostly Hating Tories

poems by
Janine Booth

For more information, poems, articles and more, visit:
www.janinebooth.com
Website design by Peter North @prnorth

For enquiries, including inviting Janine to perform her poetry,
contact **janine.booth@btopenworld.com**

Published by The Hastings Press
ISBN 978-1-904109-29-7
Book design by the author

contents

about the author

Janine Booth was a 'ranting poet' in the 1980s under the name The Big J, and after a brief break of a mere quarter-century, returned to venting her spleen on the poetic stage in summer 2014. She has performed at London poetry nights including Jawdance, Loose Muse, Technically Speaking and Paper Tiger Poetry, and at political and campaign events.

Janine's poems have been published in various journals and websites, including Poetry24, Stand Up and Spit, Solidarity, Women's Fightback and TenFootCity.

Janine is an active trade unionist, Marxist and socialist-feminist. She tutors and speaks on various political and historical subjects.

Also by Janine Booth

Guilty And Proud Of It:
Poplar's rebel councillors and guardians 1919-1926
(Merlin Press, 2009)

Plundering London Underground:
New Labour, private capital and public service 1997-2010
(Merlin Press, 2013)

Comrades And Sisters:
women and the struggle for liberation
(Workers' Liberty, 1999)

Radical Chains:
sexuality and class politics
(Workers' Liberty, 1999)

Autism In The Workplace: a handbook for trade unionists
(e-published by the Trade Union Congress, 2014)

There's no news today, not a thing's taken place
It seems rather strange, but it's really the case
The sport's uneventful, the weather is grey
The travel goes smoothly, there's no news today

The autocue's empty, the bulletin's blank
No rising inflation, no run on the bank
And UKIP's pet gobshites have nothing to say
Apologies, listeners – there's no news today

We've cancelled the headlines, rescheduled the sport
We've phoned round the regions, there's nowt to report
We just couldn't find any, try as we may
Nothing has happened – there's no news today

There's poverty, conflict, there's hunger and strife
But that isn't news – that's just everyday life
We're drowning in sunshine, so go and make hay
There's no need to worry, there's no news today

mostly hating tories

What shall I do on this fine day?
There's so much on my list
A mix of work and rest and play
I'm sure you get the gist
And maybe I will write a rhyme
But my unwritten law is
Every day I'll spend my time
Mostly hating Tories.

I'll go to work, some bills I'll pay
That's if I'm feeling rash,
To see her through to payment day
I'll lend my friend some cash,
I'll probably make my kids some tea
And read them bedtime stories
Of homeless piggies one, two, three
And why they hate the Tories.

I'll hate them for the bedroom tax
I'll hate them for the cuts,
For living off the workers' backs
I'll hate their very guts,
Look, see the depths to which they'll sink,
They don't know where the floor is,
That's why I'll spend today, I think,
Mostly hating Tories.

What's that you say? That hate's not nice?
Please love thine enemy?
Well yeah, I tried that once or twice
It doesn't work for me,
And if you think that's not fair play
Remember this, you must:
The Tories, they will spend their day
Mostly hating us.

A history of evil done
Will justify my hate,
I still detest the Tory scum
For Section Twenty Eight,
Nye Bevan built the NHS
So he knows what the score is:
And he said vermin come off best
Compared with bloody Tories.

I'm sure I'll find time to revile
That UKIP and its drivel
And I'll locate a little while
To loathe a lonesome Liberal,
I'll maybe pause to show regret
For Labour's missing glories
But save my fiercest fury yet
For mostly hating Tories.

For generations and hereon
Our class and those before us
Grew up to know which side we're on:
The side that's not the Tories,
So when I die, do this for me –
Inscribe and sing in chorus
Here lies Janine, her life spent she
Mostly hating Tories.

freudian slip

October 2014: Welfare Minister Lord Freud, replying to a councillor at a Conservative conference fringe meeting, suggested some disabled people might be exempted from the minimum wage and paid £2 per hour.

When he answered that councillor's question
   He let out a Freudian slip
When he argued for wages exemption
   It wasn't a gaffe or a blip
When his Lordship said disabled workers
   Should get by on two quid an hour
No, he wasn't just acting the jerk as
   Though he'd just come down in a shower

He was voicing his deep-seated feeling
   And saying what most Tories think
And his innermost bigot revealing –
   A slip named for Sigmund the shrink
Now the trouble he's in – give him credit –
   Is not for the vile thing he said
But merely the fact that he said it
   And didn't stay tight-lipped instead

Cos the party that's not above shutting
   The life-saving fund, ILF,
And doesn't think twice about cutting
   Back Access to Work for the deaf
Will not likely have moral objection
   To cutting our wages next June
And Lord Freud? He just needed correction
   For letting it slip out too soon

mostly hating tories

Iain Duncan Smith, Secretary of State for Work and Pensions, is Conservative MP for Chingford. The previous MP was Norman Tebbit.

What evil lurks in the deep, dark cess
Of the filthy mind of IDS?
To seek out those already poor
And find new torments to hurt them more
Requires a special sort of spite –
But I may be able to shed some light
I can exclusively reveal
That the name he goes by is not quite real
It's a shroud he uses to deceive us with
His real name's Iain Duncan *Sith*

Always there are two: Apprentice and Master
Mentored by Tebbit, Darth IDS came after
He's more machine than man, it's said
Disfigured, rebuilt, his soul long dead
Do not underestimate the power
Of the Dark Side to bring us to our darkest hour
Use the Force of mobilisation
Build a Rebel Alliance across the nation
Give in to your anger, harness your hate
Fulfil your destiny, deliver his fate
Strike down the Sith – save the Welfare State

the boris bridge

*November 2014: Conservative Mayor of London Boris Johnson
announced plans for a new 'garden bridge' across the River Thames,
run by a private company during daylight hours, with a fee to enter.*

Roll up! Roll up! for BoJo's garden bridge
We hope financial footfall will be brisk
A tourist trap for paying patronage
No groups of more than eight – a 'protest risk'
Some sixty million pounds the public pay
He raised the cash by cutting transport staff
But don't expect a public right of way
Just troubled water and a mayoral laugh
No bikes, no rights, no access after dark
Our public funds misused to privatise
It's no more than a plundered pleasure park
A Tory-governed London bridge of sighs
    A private perk like Johnson's cable car
    This really is a Boris bridge too far

sonnet to a tory mp

*A re-write of Shakespeare's
eighteenth sonnet*

Shall I compare thee to a winter's day?
Thou art more cold and more intemperate
Tough times won't shake the buddies of Theresa May
Nor cruelty's lease expire on short a date
No time too bright the lure of power shines
And never is its gold complexion dimmed
And never greed and nastiness declines
No chance your nature changes or is trimmed
But thy eternal meanness shall not fade
Nor lose possession of the wealth thou own
Nor shall the workers brag how much you're paid
When in eternal lines your expense has grown
    So long as we can breathe or eyes can see
    So long we'll live to fight the likes of thee

tory shorts

Cameron Cares?

'How very dare you suggest
I don't care for our great NHS?
I love it so dearly
I'd sell it for nearly
As much as my granny – or less'

◆◆◆

Carpe Diem

Seize the day, Theresa May,
Lock extremist scum away
While you're there, inspect the cell
And lock yourself inside as well

◆◆◆

An Ode To Jeremy Hunt

The Health Secretary's named Jeremy Hunt
He sits on the benches at front
It would, inter alia,
Insult female genitalia
To call him a vile Tory cunt

homeless man dies frozen

February 2013: Homeless man Daniel Gauntlett died of hypothermia on the doorstep of an empty bungalow in Aylesford, Kent.

Homeless man dies frozen on steps of empty bungalow
Man named Daniel Gauntlett
Headline of Kent local paper
Just words
But real death, real tragedy, real outrage

Homeless man dies frozen on steps of empty bungalow
Boards on windows and lock on door
Standing between him
And the meagre shelter that could have saved him
No bed, no luxury, no comfort
But at least a barrier between him and the murderous cold

Homeless man dies frozen on steps of empty bungalow
A person without a home
Dies on the steps of
A home without a person
In what sort of irrational system does that happen?

Someone 'owned' the empty home
And possession is not just nine-tenths of the law
But the iron law that says you can't come in
Even if it makes the difference between life and death

Homeless man dies frozen on steps of empty bungalow
It was not just the temperature that killed Daniel
It was the system
Property is not just theft
It is also murder

Daniel deserved to survive
But this system does not
Capitalism kills
Homeless man dies frozen on steps of empty bungalow

If you evade your tax when all around you
Are paying theirs and saying you should too
If values like integrity confound you
But ruthlessness comes easily to you
If you can live off other people's labour
And add their output to your growing hoard
And still proclaim yourself the wealth creator
That massive bonus is your just reward

If you can wear a smile and feign compassion
While telling men and women they are sacked
If you can pay the rest a meagre ration
That's just enough to keep them coming back
If you can welcome technical invention
So you can push more workers out the door
If ev'ry time you have the same intention:
Pay fewer people less to churn out more

If you can make one heap of all your winnings
And strive for still yet more without delay
If you can rise from not so low beginnings
And step on other people on the way
If you can treat your workers and your clients
With equal measures of detached disdain
If you can make them feel like lambs not lions
Resent each other not seek common gain

If you can buy an MP or a question
Or hire a lobby firm to do the deed
If you will pay the price of an election
Ensure the 'business' candidates succeed
If you can fill the unforgiving boardroom
With men whose moral compass points to none
Yours is the Earth and everything that's in it
And – more – you'll be a capitalist, my son!

I check my step before the food bank door
See rows of tins and people taken fright
I wish I could go back a year before

Back then my gaze had not yet sunk so poor
Still bought the thought my future might be bright
Knocked hopeful on another hirer's door

No after no, yet still I asked one more
But no-one hired, their margins were too tight
Please take me back another year before

Our boss said then that tough times were in store
Looked down and swore that he'd see us alright
But once we'd bowed he sent us through the door

I did not answer union calls to war
I told myself it wasn't worth a fight
I wish it were not now but years before

If I had known our fate I'd not ignore
Strong-voiced appeals to link arms and unite
I'd not be stepping through the food bank door
I wish with all my heart for years before

◆ ◆ ◆

Look back, look fore, look in
– Look carefully how you choose
If you fight you might not win
– If you don't you're sure to lose

peaceful haven

Guernsey's International Poetry Competition describes the island as 'a peaceful haven, not only for finance but also for writers'.

Does finance need a place to flee?
An economic refugee?
Come seeking solace by the sea?
A safe-sound island sanctuary?

Does finance crawl here penniless?
Or stride ashore flushed with success?
So it's not known at last address
When taxed to help relieve distress?

But writers choose the same repose
We dip our pens and dip our toes
On just the beach where finance goes
We write like we don't care who knows

We sing like birds and honk like geese
Disturb poor finance in its peace

terminal 420

*October 2014: a seafarer was
killed at Antwerp port while a
ship was being loaded.
The port is staffed only by
registered dockers.
The European Commission
wants to scrap rules like this;
trade unions fear this would
lead to worse safety standards
and more deaths.*

Terminal 420 is closed today
An accident happened, a sailor is dead
They have to take the body away

There's cordon and hazard tape – please go away
Don't come any nearer, there's danger ahead
Terminal 420 is closed today

The load piled up and the pile gave way
The process was safe, so the paperwork said
And now they're taking the body away

They're ticking their clipboards to work out who'll pay
They'll hold an inquiry and put it to bed
Terminal 420 is closed today

Just three deaths a year, now that figure's OK
For so busy a port: that is what the man said
After they'd taken the body away

The standard will slip if the rule doesn't stay
The Register goes, casual working instead
Terminal 420 is closed today
And soon they'll be taking more bodies away

janine booth

N38 to the world

This poem was written on a journey on the N38 night bus from Hackney to St. Pancras, London, and then on to the Eurostar.

I used to but I haven't missed this bus
At 5a.m., a half-full cart to take
The staff who clean and guard before you wake
Who start the engines 'fore the rest of us
From brief repose unwilling exodus
Hold open half-mast eyes on work-worn faces
Resignedly wishing they weren't going places
No chat, no caucus, nothing to discuss
But then I disembark and change my routes
And switch dimensions through a boarding gate
Some two hours later morning, bright debate
White, coffee-charged commuters sporting suits
    While most of those on night bus 38
    Were black and wearing hi-vis, smocks and boots

mostly hating tories

death row diner

September 2014: Following protests, organisers cancelled the pop-up restaurant 'Death Row Dinners', planned to run in Hoxton the following month with a menu of prisoners' last meals.

May I invite you to my cell to dine?
Is this the final meal that you will face?
It's Hoxton's newest, sickest hipster line
For those about to die salute your taste
Sit down in your unplugged electric chair
There's extra seats for people black or poor
Our bar sells lethal shots and grilled despair
Please give your racial profile at the door
Come join the fun, you hipster boys and gals
Try innocents condemned with clotted cream
We don't suppose you're counting kilo-cals
That really wouldn't fit in with the theme
    At fifty quid, it's cheap at twice the price
    It's pop-up cos you sure can't eat here twice

the ballad of gibbons corner

Since Eighteen Ninety
In all of its finery
Stood Gibbons the furniture sellers
London's last such attraction
With cash-only transaction
Until plastic caught up with the fellas

They eventually gave in
To modernity's whim
With a sign saying 'We accept Visa'
Through bombings and raids
Gibbons still stayed
Hackney's very own Tower of Pisa

The long coat of a draper
The colour of brown paper
Archetypal shopkeeper of Britain
In the top pocket a pen
Just waiting for when
A receipt would need to be written

It was stocked up with lots
Of toys, prams and cots
Gibbons the finest purveyors
But the Victorian store
Sells furniture no more
And now attracts only surveyors

There, I bought my boy
An ironing board toy
He wanted to help out indoors
(This is only a stage
Which ends at the age
When they're capable of doing the chores)

mostly hating tories

The block first begun
In Eighteen Thirty One
Before the Poor Law and good Queen Victoria
By the turn of Two Thousand
A clothes shop it housed, and
Bars, café and Gibbons emporia

And the Earl of Amherst pub
Which sold booze but not grub
And saw many an evening of laughter
Where dogs were allowed
Until we took our hound
And dogs weren't permitted thereafter

In Two Thousand and Three
We returned from the sea
To find Gibbons was totally gutted
The previous night, it
Mysteriously ignited
Hackney-watchers collectively tutted

For many a week
The ash and smoke reeked
And some people also smelled rat
When at auction it was offered
No bids had been proffered
It's mighty suspicious, is that

For years behind boards
Gibbons stood there, ignored
While buddleia grew in the gaps
It could have been rebuilt
Rather than left there to wilt
As a community facility, perhaps

Once, a car park appeared
When a chap with a beard
Put a sign up and took people's money
He'd collected a lot
When the Council said 'Stop –
That's our job and we don't find it funny'

While developers schemed
In Twenty Thirteen
Gibbons Corner faced ruin once more
Damp rose and cracks grew
You could hear the trains through
And the cellar collapsed under the floor

Tenants got out alive
And the frontage survived
Saved by a timely alert
Now there's scaffolded ceiling
And you can't shake the feeling
There are two types of hoarding at work

That put paid to a scheme
A profiteers' dream
Of a Travelodge eighty-bed dormer
A 'cheap' place to crash
Built on the ash
And the embers of old Gibbons Corner

The abyss round the back
Displays a huge crack
Like the one in Amelia Pond's wall
And like in Doctor Who
It's time seeping through
Running out for the old shopping mall

Like Ground Zero the view
That you're welcomed to
As you disembark at the station
(But without the world's press
Or the thousands of deaths
Or the war of retaliation)

Hackney folk walk on by
Not a flick of the eye
Not a moment's attention to give
It's nothing too weird
That a crater's appeared
In the midst of the place where we live

But visitors gasp
As they stop still and ask
'What site of calamity is that?'
Then, 'Which way, actually
To the Burberry factory?'
Presumably to buy a nice hat

After fire, collapse or riot
Our neighbourhood goes quiet
As they close Amhurst Road off to traffic
It's calm and it's still
You can walk where you will
The contrast is really quite graphic

The deserted road space is
An urban oasis
It's a wonder we never played cricket
The tarmac terrain
And the white-paint-lined lanes
Would have marked out a marvellous wicket

The traffic's diverted
And bus number thirty
Announces its next stopping port
But check your assumption
Of the name of this junction
It's probably not what you thought

What all Hackney says
Is called the Five Ways
Is suddenly named Pembury Circus
Could this be a new
Entertainment venue
Provided by clowns for the workers?

No. It happens to be
The name of the block you can see
Of new flats and shops where the grass is
(Or was.) Did the developer pay
For this branded display
Or get given the advert for gratis?

To show us they care
They boldly declare
That 'affordable housing' has risen
But when fifty per cent
Is affordable to rent
That means fifty per cent of it isn't

Next door, a closed college
Where on the rubble of knowledge
A wit from the Naming Department
In a sad, mocking troll
Of its previous role
Called it Academy Apartments

It costs over a million
For a three-bedroom brilliant-
-ly decorated and located flat
With classrooms now bedrooms
There's plenty of headroom
And widthroom for swinging a cat

You'll love the location
It's right near the station
Just a quick hop and skip from the door
You can commute to the City
And get to it pretty
Much without tripping over the poor

Round the corner from there
A home for youth leaving care
Lies demolished – new usage awaits
And where once stood facilities
For kids with disabilities
There now stand flats behind gates

But our estate stands
Untouched by the hands
Of the area's property vultures
They had numerous plans
To 'develop' the land
Replace our homes with money-shrine sculptures

What consideration
For the estate's population
While developers slavered and panted?
They employed wit and wisdom
In a great euphemism
When they told us we would be 'decanted'

Home-owners and tenants
Raised banners and pennants
And proclaimed our estate Not For Sale
And when more vultures swooped
Our campaign regrouped
And made sure the bastards turned tail

Now Gibbons old shops
Are held up by props
I guess in more than one sense
The façade is still there
It shows that they care
It keeps up a civic pretence

What new incarnation
What monstrous creation
Will rise from the ashes and dust?
We can be sure
That whatever it's for
Will be them and their profits, not us

If there's one thing to learn
From events and their turn
From fire, collapse, ash, dust and powder
It's the strong not the meek
And the money will speak
Unless our community speaks louder

He tells us what to think and do
And shouts until the air turns blue
Then when he's done enlightening folk
He goes outside and has a smoke
She bites her lip and lifts her hand
Says 'I'm not sure I understand
I'm probably wrong but anyway …'
And makes the best point made all day

money for the dunny

I'm writing this verse on the toilet
A priv'lege that cost me the Earth
Forty p for to pee is an outrage
I'm determined to use all it's worth

I'll sit on the throne 'til my train comes
It's a platform, and I'm in no rush
They are piping departure announcements
Through a speaker that's next to the flush

I will get my value for money
For this bog and the time I spend in it
If I stay here until fourteen fifty
Then that will be one p a minute

They're taking the piss with these charges
It's not even half price unwaged
The neighbouring cubicle's vacant
But the one that I'm sat in's enraged

I'm making a stand with my sit-in
My protest is now on a roll
But the minutes of khazi confinement
Will soon start extracting their toll

It's a product of privatised privies
The malodorous stench of the system
So I'll keep on composing my poem
Then publish it here, on the cistern

Now I've nearly finished my rhyming
And then I'll be tweeting and typing
If you're finding this image distasteful
Just be grateful that I am not Skyping

sonnet to the domestic dog

There is a fact scarce known in our society
That of the world's great treasury of creatures
The one that manifests the most variety
Of size and shape and other body features
Is not a lizard, rabbit or a cat
Nor common toad nor more uncommon frog
It's not a shrew or mouse or vole or rat
It's our best friend, much-loved domestic dog
It's black, white, brown, grey, even red like setters
From shaggy sheepdog to the Chinese hairless
From those where breeders really should know better
To marvellous mongrels mating free and careless
    But tell me why if this should be the case
    They share the same daft look upon their face?

janine booth

the jeremy kyle nativity rap

We've had a call from Joseph down in Royal David's City
His fiancée's had a baby – but now things aren't looking pretty
We've heard some crazy stories in this studio before
But when they told me this one, well it really dropped my jaw
This'll be a new direction for our famous lie detection
'My girlfriend said she's pregnant through immaculate conception'
Welcome Joseph on the stage, he's feeling pretty daft
Tell us all that happened – from the very start
They said we had to register, get papers with our name on
Had to leave our home 'hood and go back to where we came from
Jumped into a lorry with a star on the side
Bumped us like a donkey, what a nasty ride
The hostels couldn't cope and the Council wouldn't help
They told us there's a bloke who could probably sort us out
'Through that wooden door – Mind the Headroom, Max
We re-labelled it a stable for the Bedroom Tax'

Getting merry in style with some daytime TV crap
It's the Jeremy Kyle Nativity Rap!
Getting merry in style with some daytime TV crap
It's the Jeremy Kyle Nativity Rap!

She had the baby in that room and everything seemed fine
But when we went to register, she said it wasn't mine
Came up with a fable – really quite a strange tale
Some guy called Gabriel – said he was an angel
Told her he was sent to her to save the world
But I reckon that he says that to all the girls
Next on stage it's Gabe – I can't wait to hear this
Stay low or his halo'll have another near miss
'Joseph's only saying this so he can get away
With claiming that the kid's not his so he don't have to pay
Trying to run away from the C.S.A.
Two millennia too early to test D.N.A.

mostly hating tories

You wanna watch out I don't smack you, mate
Your girlfriend said our hook-up was immaculate'
Let's hear what the mother says – Mary's on the phone
'They're both as bad as each other, Jez – I'm better off on my own'

Sipping sherry, spitting bile, now they're itching for a scrap
It's the Jeremy Kyle Nativity Rap!
Sipping sherry, spitting bile, now they're itching for a scrap
It's the Jeremy Kyle Nativity Rap!

It's J.C.'s birthday – and M.C. J.K.
Tells it how it is – and this is what they say
Want to name and shame and blame? Well, this is not conducive
The all-important lie detector came back inconclusive
Think you are an angel? – I think you are a slob
Get off your lazy backside and get yourself a job!
Babies don't come cheap, you know – you're going to have to
    spend a bit
Bet you end up wishing you'd put something on the end of it
We're gonna give you help from the aftercare team
They're busy at the minute in a rehab scheme
Got a spot of bother finding three wise men
But it's nice to give advice and so we'll see you guys then
We'll be back soon with more shocking revelations
Adam wants the truth about his lover's temptations
Make sure you don't leave – join us after the break
Find out whether Eve was hit on by a snake

There's at least an eight mile credibility gap
It's the Jeremy Kyle Nativity Rap!
There's at least an eight mile credibility gap
It's the Jeremy Kyle Nativity Rap!

two women every week

In England and Wales, women are killed by current or former male partners at the rate of two a week. Thanks to Count Dead Women for its work in telling these truths.

One hour in every eighty-four
Another body hits the floor
A hundred women every year
Killed by one they once held dear
Nine a month, four a fortnight
Do these figures sound too forthright?
The facts have faces, truth will speak
– Two women every week

Life's moved since seven days ago
The weekends fast, the weekdays slow
Your seven sleeps and wakes since then
Saw two more women's living end
At hands of those who hands they'd hold
Who held their trust 'til trust turned cold
An open-ended killing streak
– Two women every week

Lisa, Gemma, Jade, Chantelle,
Poonam, Debbie, Yvonne, Janelle,
Sarah, Hollie, Kate, Sameena,
Kanwal, Sandra, Anne, Madina,
Reece bashed Ashley round the head,
David stabbed Linah, now she's dead
Their daughter saw and heard her shriek
– Two women every week

mostly hating tories

Count dead women, name the missing
Mark every death, 'til people listen
Some stalked by those who can't accept
That's she's moved on; he won't respect
'Cos she was his, possessed by man
If he can't have her, no-one can
Deadly hunt, she hides, he seeks
– Two women every week

So where's the headline, where's the rage?
Why's this not on your front page?
If there's a hook that grabs attention
Maybe her murder merits mention
Model slaughtered, beauty slain
Psycho monster loose again
Otherwise, it's just not news
– Our women dead, our ones and twos

The time has passed for being meek
– Two women every week
The time has come for us to speak
– Two women every week
Take action now cos talk is cheap
– Two women every week
We will not let this matter sleep
– Two women every week

Two women every week.

real rape

If she's drunk or she's flirty
Or a boozy young floozy
If she likes talking dirty
If she isn't that choosy
If she touched him or kissed him
And she then changed her mind
If she's scared to resist him
If she liked it last time
If most everyone knows
That she usually says yes
If she shows off her toes
If she wears a tight dress
If she's not in great shape
Then it's not really rape
– Is it?

If the guy is her boyfriend
If they're out on a date
If they shared some enjoyment
If they stayed up quite late
If he's rich or he's famous
Or a top football star
Well that's not quite the same, that's
Just going too far
If the man is convicted
But he keeps on denying
Says it's wrongly depicted
And his girlfriend stands by him
If his name's in the paper
Then he didn't really rape her
– Did he?

mostly hating tories

If the girl never fought it
Or she lay still and cowered
If she didn't report it
Until after she'd showered
If she didn't speak out
Until months or years later
Then there's reasonable doubt
About this perpetrator
And if nobody saw
And if nobody heard
Then you need something more
Than just that woman's word
With no videotape
Then it's not really rape
– Is it?

If it gets to a court
We'll explain to the jury
That we all know her sort
You know, hell hath no fury
She's just angry and bitter
Cos he's dumped her and left
And it's not like he hit her
She's just sad and bereft
If she's mentally ill
Then you cannot believe her
She's forgotten her Pill
She is scared that he'll leave her
It's a trick, lie or jape
But it's not really rape
- Is it?

It's not really rape
It's just bad bedroom manners
It's not really rape
She's just trying to scam us
'It's not rape', says a shirt
'It's a snuggle with a struggle'
She is not really hurt
She's just trying to cause trouble
It's not really a crime
It's another blurred line
You know men don't have time
To decode every sign
On the sexual landscape
So it's not really rape
- Is it?

Real rape takes place
In a poorly-lit lane
With a mask on the face
Of a man who's insane
Real rape's committed
By sick monsters with knives
And by psychos and rippers
Not by ordinary guys
Real rape victims are angels
They're sober and chaste
They're jumped on by strangers
They report it post haste
And they try to escape
We accept that's real rape

Please let's stop making out
There are some rapes worth less
Or they somehow don't count
As the slogans will stress
That wherever we go
And however we dress
The word 'no' still means no
Only 'yes' can mean yes
If she says neither word
Or you can't really tell
Then she hasn't concurred
And so that's 'no' as well
It's consent seals the deal –
And without it, rape's real.

her name is reeva

Her name is Reeva
Reeva Steenkamp
Not 'Oscar Pistorius's girlfriend'
Not 'model'
Not 'reality TV star'
Her name is Reeva

Her name is Reeva
Reeva Steenkamp
She was not just a model
But also a law graduate
She was not just a reality TV star
But also a campaigner against violence
This story is about her killing
Not about his fame
Or it ought to be
Her name is Reeva

His name is Oscar
Oscar Pistorius
And every news report calls him that
Her name is Reeva
Reeva Steenkamp –
Sometimes mentioned
But only after 'his model girlfriend'

He slept with guns
She is one of fifty victims of homicide every day in South Africa

Her name is Reeva
She is a woman
A person in her own right
Not an appendage of the celebrity who killed her
Even in death
She still has a name
Use it please.

mostly hating tories

the housewife's trial

Your Honour, I'm only a poor housewife
And the one great joy in my boring life
Is to get my laundry white and clean
The light of my life is my washing machine

So this morning I had a terrible shock
'Cos the dirt said hot but the label said not
With the stains on his undies and the dirt on his vest
They'll never pass the window test
It really did come as a terrible fright
I'll never get them bluey-white
My powder's so crap I'm sure that it won't
Shift those stubborn stains that ordinary non-biological powders don't

Then all of a sudden, to allay my fears
A man in a long white coat appeared
He said 'It's new, it's improved, it's the best you can buy
It's fuckin' amazing, why not give it a try?'
Then more appeared and very soon
Washing powder salesman filled up the room
But under all that pressure my patience snapped
And in the soap powder advert, the housewife strikes back!

I attacked 'em all with piano wire
Put their heads in the machine and their bodies in the drier
I grabbed 'em by the willies and pulled 'em through the mangle
I spun 'em and wrung 'em until they were strangled
Then I washed 'em and rinsed 'em a couple more times
Hung 'em up by the bollocks from the washing line
I took 'em down and shook 'em to get rid of their crinkles
Put 'em on the ironing board and ironed out their wrinkles

I didn't mean to kill 'em – it was out of frustration
I was sick of being subjected to their patronisation
So I stand accused Your Honour of this terrible offence
And the one thing I can say is – it was in self defence!

janine booth

my friend hush

*I wrote this poem in support of Rainbow
International LGBT Activist Solidarity Fund's
campaign in support of Hush Ainebyona.*

My friend Hush is good and kind
And fair and just – and going blind

From boy to woman, Hush had grown
Rejection, hatred always known
My friend Hush tried to escape
A cycle of abuse and rape
Went to college, couldn't stay
Worked Kampala's streets for pay

My friend Hush went to meet a friend
But the friend brought a friend and a nasty end
My friend Hush was pushed to the floor
And punched and kicked and punched some more
My friend Hush cried out in vain
As her eyes filled up with blood and pain

Hush hid out for two long days
Away from the thugs' and bigots' gaze
When Hush told police of this crime of hate
They didn't bother to investigate
And only certain doctors treat
A social outcast, badly beat

Now my friend Hush is going blind
As blind as the prejudice in those small, mean minds
And the government that stands behind
Politics and prejudice, the ties that bind
I have too many poems about hate crimes
That's too many crimes, not too many rhymes

But Hush, don't worry, you have friends
From round the globe, support extends
Hush, my friend, you are not alone
If you could see the love you're shown
Strength in common, not charity
For surgery and solidarity

My friend Hush will see once more
Stand proud against the bigots' law
My friend Hush is brave and wise
We'll open my friend Hush's eyes
We'll battle, campaign, speak out and tell –
And open Uganda's eyes as well

horseplay

*June 2012: 18-year-old, gay, autistic student Steven Simpson was killed
when gatecrashers at his party bullied and set fire to him. Sentencing
the ringleader to just 3½ years, the judge called the killing 'horseplay'.*

I heard the local judge was having a party at his flat
I thought that sounded tasty, I'll have a bit of that
There'll probably be some posh nosh and a bit of legal chat
I hadn't been invited, but who cares about that?

So I gatecrashed his little soiree, got stuck in to the grub
Nattered with the judicial types, drank champers in the tub
It certainly beat another night down our dingy local pub
But then it got a bit out of hand and therein lies the rub

I got talking to His Honour – he seemed a decent sort
Regaling us with stories of happy days in court
But then he got on to a case which left me so distraught
A young lad's murder was 'horseplay' or so the scumbag thought

'If poofs and weirdos must have parties, what do they expect?
When normal people turn up, they're certain to object
No need to be excessive, the sentence is correct
A couple of years inside, a short while to reflect'

I thought I'd have some horseplay, so tore off his wig and gown
Scrawled 'judge boy' on his body and 'I like sending people down'
I doused him in oil and champers and set light to the clown
Then ran away while others tried to smother the flames down

I didn't mean to kill him – it was good-natured horseplay
My defence brief calls it 'a stupid prank that went wrong in a bad way'
So I think I'll be alright in court, get a shortish prison stay
And unlike my poor victim, get to party again some day

mostly hating tories

no autistics here

July 2014: Plans to set up a care home for
autistic adults on a street in Swindon were
abandoned following objections by residents.

No autistics in our neighbourhood
We just don't want those weirdo freaks around
We'd stop them moving in here if we could

We're normal folk, don't tell us to do good
We pay our rates of several thousand pound
For no autistics in our neighbourhood

You'd say the same in our shoes, yes you would
Our need to circle wagons is profound
We'd stop them moving in here if we could

We want our so-called reasons understood
We'll think of some; we're sure they will be sound
For no autistics in our neighbourhood

Small minds are made up, hostile ground is stood
Our empathy is lost, our coldness found
We'd stop them moving in here if we could

Perhaps we'll don a white robe and a hood
Let loose the NIMBYs and their baying hound
Bark no autistics in our neighbourhood
We stopped them moving in because we could

mood swings

Bright skies, natural highs,
Summer haze, happy days,
Good things ... mood swings

Dark cloud, not proud
Guilt, shame, down again
Life's shit, deep pit
Break down, sink, drown,
Gasp for air, nothing there,
No hope, can't cope
Tunnel light out of sight
Ranting, railing, falling, failing

Life's exciting, life is frightening
Life is thrilling, pressure's killing
Life's a breeze, life's on its knees
One hour flying, next one crying

How now, selfish cow
Just pull yourself together now
Damn and curse your indulgent verse
Others cope with much much worse
Depression bout? Leave it out!
Don't know what the fuss is about

Knives. Forks. Spoons. Obviously.
What other arrangement could it possibly be?
There's a reason that cutlery drawers have three distinct spaces -
So we can place our utensils in their correct places
That's forks in the middle, knives and spoons to their border
How could you entertain any other order?!
And the little slot, sideways, at the front of the drawer
Is for teaspoons – what else could it be for?!
The long berth up the side – the clue is: it's long
It's for long stuff, like a carving knife, skewer or barbecue prong

Knives. Forks. Spoons. Self-evidently.
What mind-meddling mischief are you playing with me?
Forks, spoons, knives – never! It would make me so cross
But not quite as cross as the untargeted toss
Of cutlery cast casually to wherever it may fall
Spoons in the knife slot or in no slot at all
I'm going to have to use some labels
For things that may be laid on tables
I place things correctly, even if some folk can't
It's not because I'm autistic – it's because other people aren't

janine booth   41

B104-82

When an officer was killed in World War One, the British Army told his next ↕ kin by telegram. Lower-ranked men's deaths were reported on Form B104–8. 'Calamity' is a poem by E.H. Visiak. Private Ted was my great uncle.

Visiak's Calamity once said
From heart to heart grief's wireless sped
No officer, this Hoxton lad
No telegram to mum and dad
Grief's letters only slowly plod
Five weeks through Flanders' shell-churned sod
'Til death's cold-morning cockerel crowed
Outside a house on Edgware Road
Five weeks false hope for Private Ted
At last they learned their son was dead

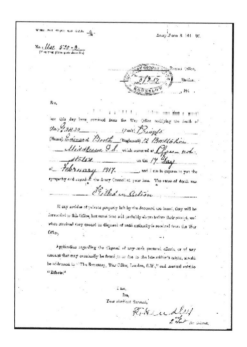

mostly hating tories

sonnet for shahrokh and reza

*Shahrokh Zamani and Reza Shahabi
are imprisoned in Iran for
organising trade unions.*

They hold in prison those whom power fears
Shahrokh and Reza, Rajai Shahr's closed doors
Lock up these men but can't lock up their cause
Starved, beaten, tortured, jailed eleven years
Iran's regime: the workers' enemy
It stole the revolution 'gainst the Shah
Now everywhere in chains its people are
Lash-bound by theocratic tyranny
Hang men from cranes for loving other men
Cruel punish women who have been abused
Most basic rights to unionise refused
Freedom's question is not 'if?' But 'when?'
    The workers of the world will set them free
    And break these bars with solidarity

burning out?

When my mum was my age I'd moved out
– That makes me old

When I stumble and ache and feel doubt
– That makes me tired

When I still see injustice and pain
– That makes me hold

On to anger and all that's humane
– That makes me fired

Up for the fight.
Still.